"I love the practicality of each tool. Many survivors of trauma do not know where to start in order for their healing process to begin. In this book, survivors learn to approach their healing one step at a time."

—Chanté Dent,
Founder of Earnest Love, Inc.

"... an essential and compact resource book that one can refer back to over and over again... The easy-to-follow layout, quotes, blank "notes" section and the variety of personal narratives from survivors provides the reader the freedom to supplement the book as a journal or spiritual guide... it is definitely created for US."

—Jodie Ortega,
Breaking My Silence

"...a very important tool that is easy to follow and understand... Every survivor just transitioning out of the trauma into freedom should be equipped with a tool like this. Had I been aware resources like this were available after I left my abuser of over 4 years, the first year would have been much easier to handle."

— Amy

GW00776882

11 TOOLS TO HELP MANAGE
THE AFTERMATH OF
TRAUMA

TIFFANI DILWORTH,
MA, LCPC

11 Tools to Help Manage the Aftermath of Trauma
Copyright © 2016 by Inspirational Hope LLC. All rights
reserved. Printed in the United States of America.

Editor Shavonya Coleman
Cover Design by Crystal Manu

Ordering Information: Quantity sales. Special discounts
are available on quantity purchases by corporations,
associations, and others. For details, contact
Inspirational Hope, LLC at the below address:
P.O. Box 3651
Silver Spring, MD 20918
Or visit www.InspirationalHope.org

ISBN 978-1-329-96604-8

Dedication

To anyone who's experienced a trauma. This book
was written for the sole purpose of you, the reader.
I pray each of you find something in this book that
helps you progress in your journey to leading a
healthier and more successful life.

I thank my family for their love and support. I thank
all of the people who played a role in making this
book a success. I thank all of my friends for their
encouragement. I thank all the people who have
come in and out of my life for a season and for the
opportunity I had to learn many life lessons.

Most of all, I thank God for all that He's done for me.
I thank Him for life and new opportunities to grow
closer to Him each day.

Contents

Preface

11Tools to Help Manage the Aftermath of Trauma is a book that has coping skills from different theoretical orientations that many counselors use in therapy sessions today. It's encouraged that you read the entire book through and find which ones work for you. The tools shared are only a starting point to help in your journey to healing after abuse. We are all in a different place in our journey, so you'll find that some are helpful while others aren't, and that's okay. Everything doesn't work for everyone. Find what works for you.

The tools are listed alphabetically. In each chapter, you will find the name of the tool or technique to manage your symptoms. You will also see **Benefits** which will describe what symptoms of trauma it may help to reduce. Next, a description of the tool or technique will be given. You will find a **What to do** section in each chapter. This section provides a step-by-step plan on how to use the tool described. Some chapters have examples of how to implement the tool discussed. At the end of each chapter, you will also find a **Notes** section where you will be able to write down anything that will support you in your journey to reaching a healthier and more successful life.

Keep in mind that dealing with the aftermath of trauma takes time to work through. If you have a mental health therapist, it's encouraged to let them know which tools in this book you found to be helpful so they can further support you in your healing journey. If you don't have a counselor and feel that you need further help, it's encouraged to speak with a professional

counselor for further support.

Chapter One

Evaluate Your Mindset Game

Benefits: Reduce Flashbacks, Redirect Anger, Redirect Anxiety

It's easy to get stuck in the past. We can become trapped in a wormhole of memories. Has anyone ever told you, "Yes, it happened; doesn't mean you have to think about it. So just stop thinking about it," or "It happened a long time ago, let it go," or maybe even, "That's all you talk about, get over it." All of those statements have a bit of truth to them. Don't believe me? Let's take another look.

"Yes, it happened....It happened a long time ago...that's all you talk about." These components of the statements may be are true and are in a way, comforting because the other person is acknowledging that something bad has happened. What's disheartening and at times disappointing are the words they choose to show their frustration, "doesn't mean you have to think about it...let it go...get over it."

Loved ones who tell us to "just get over it," don't understand that if we could jump out of this tormenting wormhole of memories, we would. Don't they get that we didn't like living through the actual trauma, and definitely don't like reliving it over and over and over again in our heads? Don't they understand that we feel helpless in this never-ending wormhole of memories and if we could change it, we would?

I have a secret for you. Well, it's not really a secret; it's actually something that has been with us since we were born. It's called a secret because many of us have lost, misplaced, or simply forgotten this tool. The best way to describe it is to go back to the beginning.

Have you ever just sat and watched a baby explore the world around them? They move from object to object, placing any and everything into their mouth to learn more about it. Sometimes, the baby will get a hold of an object and is reluctant to let go of it. It's as if something inside of them is telling them, "You want this, you need this, you can't let it go." It's surprising what a strong grip some babies have when they don't want to give up an object. Sure they fuss and whine, some even cry for an extend period of time, but the majority usually can be comforted by being entertained with another object or activity.

When we have continual flashbacks or traumatic nightmares, it's like our brain is telling us, "Hey, I've been altered, you have to think about the trauma."

The same way the baby cried until they were entertained with something else, we go through the same difficult and frustrating process of changing how our brain works to reach the point of rarely or never experiencing flashbacks or traumatic nightmares.

The things we use to "entertain" ourselves with are goals. It may seem strange, but keep reading, it'll make sense. If we view our life as a game where there is a goal we are trying to reach, we might be surprised at how successful we will be in reducing our flashbacks and traumatic nightmares.

Let's take a deeper look at what all goes into playing a game. Check out **What to do** section in order to start taking back control of your brain and being successful in winning the game.

What to do:

1. First, you need a team. This would be your support system. (a friend, significant other, family member, God, etc.)

2. Identify a meaningful goal. A few examples would be becoming active in the PTA, getting a job, getting your driver's license, writing a book, learning to cook, losing weight, learning to dance, etc.

3. Do things every day to reach your goal, even if it's as small as locating a dance studio and finding out the cost,

or creating an outline for a book you're going to write.

4. Do regular check-ins with where you are in reaching your goals. It can be daily, weekly, or monthly check-ins. By doing this, life seems easier to handle because you have a direction you're going in, a destination you're striving to reach.

5. When you check-in, list the areas you've done well in and the areas that you can improve in. It's vital that you are honest with yourself.

6. After you've done something good in a game, what do you do? You celebrate! So after your check-ins, celebrate the areas you've done well in. It's

important that you acknowledge your growth and successes.

7. If there are areas of growth, adjust yourself based on your evaluation. So you may choose to cook more often, or do more research on how to publish your own book.

8. If we get stuck in a game, what do we oftentimes do? We ask for help. If you feel stuck or a lack of motivation, go back to number one and find someone in your support system who can help you out. Their help can be along the lines of attending a cooking class with you because you don't want to go alone, or you tell them about your book idea to get their thoughts and suggestions.

9. Stay focused on the goal you set. If flashbacks happen, go back to the goal you set in number two, and writeljlkjl down ways you can reach it.

Notes

_____

_____

_____

_____

_____

_____

_____

Chapter Two

Express Gratitude

Benefits: Reduce Anger, Reduce Anxiety, Reduce Depression, Manage Unhealthy Thoughts, Decrease Stress Level.

Throughout my career, I've had the opportunity to conduct several depression and anxiety groups. At the end of each group meeting, we would go around the room, sharing a coping tool we were going to do that next week. The following week, several people would come back and share how they used their coping tool. It quickly became noticeable that several group members forgot to use the coping tool. We decided that at the end of each group meeting, we would do a coping tool together. We would read a list of coping tools and they would agree on one. One that was chosen time and time again was "Name something or someone you are thankful for." It quickly became a favorite.

One day I asked the group why they liked expressing gratitude so much and their responses were priceless. Several said it made the rest of their day calmer and more peaceful. Others said it reminded them that there were some good things happening in their life which gave them hope that they could have the life they were working towards creating. I can recall one person in particular said it made his outlook on life brighter because he knew that something was going good in his life and that not all of his life was bad.

In several group meetings, we would literally spend the entire meeting writing thank-you cards to people we appreciated.

In Dr. Soja Lyubomirsky's, *The How of Happiness,* she shares with us that we have 40% of the control needed to increase our level of happiness. She explains how the other 60% of our tendency to experience happiness is related to our set of genetics and our environment or life experiences.[2]

Keep in mind that 40% of our happiness is literally based on what we choose to do. If we are filled with anger, anxiety, or experiencing depression, according to research, there are things we can do to increase our happiness, and being grateful is one of them.

Dr. Lyubomirsky goes on to share that being grateful has many benefits. Benefits including raising our self-esteem and self-value, helping us cope with stress and trauma, strengthening existing relationships, reducing comparing ourselves to others, and many more benefits, not to mention health improvement.

Gratitude is an activity that benefits those who have experienced trauma because it gives an opportunity to put those negative thoughts, negative feelings, and hurtful memories away for a moment. Anger and gratitude cannot exist at the same time. Gratitude and negative thoughts cannot exist at the same time. Stress and gratitude cannot exist at the same time. When we are in the moment of expressing gratitude, only gratitude exist and the feelings associated with it, including peace, joy, and contentment.

What to do:

There are many ways to show gratitude, below are a few:

1. Keep a gratitude journal.

2. Write a letter or short note to someone who you are grateful for and give it to them.

3. Send an e-mail or text letting someone know why you appreciate them.

4. Write yourself a letter, telling yourself why you like you.

5. Give someone a hug and tell them why you are grateful for them.

If you didn't see an option that fits who you are, I encourage you to find your own way of showing gratitude to increase your level of happiness.

It's also encouraged to acknowledge how it feels to show appreciation to others.

Notes

_____

_____

_____

_____

_____

_____

_____

_____

_____

_____

Chapter 3

Grounding

Benefits: Reduce Flashbacks, Manage Negative Thoughts, Reduce Length of Panic Attacks

Grounding is one of my favorite techniques. It brings immediate results for many people. Throughout my years of counseling, I've only met a few people it hasn't worked for, a couple of whom said they forgot to try.

Grounding is extremely simple and can be done anywhere, anytime. The same way flashbacks happen or negative thoughts happen within our mind, grounding can also be done within our mind. Panic attacks are also an opportunity for us to use grounding. Although you have to have a lot of control over your mind to use grounding during a panic attack, it can be done.

You're probably thinking, "Okay, so tell us what this grounding is all about!" No problem. Grounding is a technique that brings us back to the present moment by using our senses. In Chapter Ten, we focus on the sense of touch to manage the effects of trauma. In this chapter we'll primarily focus on the sense of sight.

Take a look at this list of questions and after these questions, I'll explain grounding further:

What color is the wall?

What color is the floor?

What color is my shirt?

What color are my shoes?

What color are my socks?

What year is it?

What is today's date?

What time is it?

Who is the president or prime minister?

If you notice, all of these questions are neutral and most people are able to answer them. Asking ourselves these simple questions gives our mind an opportunity to refocus.

Sometimes our thoughts can treat us like a runaway air balloon that's high in the sky, out of our control. Asking ourselves these questions brings us back down to the ground slowly and safely. It calms our anxious feelings, our intense flashbacks, or our negative thoughts. It gives our mind a chance to redirect our thoughts.

Think of it as how a train switches train tracks to go in a different direction. It's the same concept. Someone has to switch the tracks over. In this case, answering those questions is the "switching over" moment.

Once you've answered the questions and recognized that your negative thoughts, flashbacks, or panic attack have decreased, you can do one of two things: Do an activity that will keep your mind engaged, or give yourself a pat on the back for gaining control of your mind.

It's recommended that you explore reasons why the flashbacks or panic attacks happened. Don't try to figure it out immediately (we wouldn't want your flashbacks, anxiety, or panic attack to return), but maybe a few moments later, a few hours later, or even a few days later. But be sure to take a moment to understand what triggered the panic attack or a flashback. Be sure you do it in a safe environment with your coping tools handy, just in case the flashbacks come pouring in again or a panic attack happens. You can also speak to your

Therapist about what happened and they will be able to help you figure out the trigger. Later on, we'll go into details about triggers. Triggers are sometimes easy to figure out, sometimes they're hard to figure out, and other times there seems to be no trigger at all.

What to do:

1. (Optional) Write down a list of grounding questions in a notebook, on your phone, or a 3x5 card that you can keep with you at all times.

2. Acknowledge that you are having a panic attack, flashback, or negative thought.

3. Identify colors in the room by saying, "The table is blue. The door is brown. The wall is off-white. Etc..." If you can't remember the

questions to answer, pull out the list you created in number one.

4. Remind yourself that you are in a safe place and redirect your thoughts to something positive or engage in a relaxing activity.

5. A few moments, hours, or days later, explore triggers that lead to the flashbacks, negative thoughts, or panic attacks.

Notes

_____

_____

_____

_____

_____

_____

_____

_____

_____

_____

Chapter Four

Listing triggers

Benefits: Decrease Frequency of the Following: Flashbacks, Negative Thoughts, Panic Attacks, High Anxiety, Depression, Anger

We talked about triggers briefly in the grounding technique, but here, we will talk about triggers in greater detail. First, let's start by defining a trigger. Trigger has several definitions. In this discussion, the word trigger is used as a verb, so it's an action word. Knowing that it's an action word is important and will be further explained in a moment.

According to Webster's Dictionary, a trigger means "to cause something to start or happen." Webster's Dictionary gives several examples of the word trigger, one of them being, "Certain foods trigger his headaches."[3]

Here's another example: when pollen is in the air, it triggers allergies for some people, resulting in sneezing, runny noses, and puffy eyes.

It's the same with trauma. When we experience a traumatic event, a trigger can cause us to react a certain way. A trigger can be something we see on TV, a person we see, a type of touch, a sound, a smell, or even reading an article in a magazine. Once we are triggered, it may seem like we are not in control of our reactions, and our reactions can vary. We can experience flashbacks, anxiety, depression, stuttering, and many other reactions.

So does that mean we always avoid our triggers and live in constant alertness? No. Initially, it may be healthy to avoid our triggers. As time goes on and we develop coping tools to control our reactions, those triggers seem less powerful, resulting in us having a very mild reaction to the trigger.

Let's take a look at Stephanie. Stephanie is a survivor of domestic violence from her childhood and majority of her adult life. She experienced panic attacks and depression regularly. After several years of therapy, she was able to identify her triggers and found coping tools that worked for her.

One of Stephanie's triggers was being around men who had a deep voice. At first, her panic attacks seemed random, but after exploration, she realized one of the triggers was a man's deep voice because it reminded her of her father's voice and ex-husband's voice when they would get drunk. When she left her abusive relationship and started her recovery process, fear would run through her body when she heard a man talking who had a deep voice, resulting in her experiencing a panic attack.

Once she realized that a deep voice was a trigger for her, she was able to start using coping tools more effectively. At first, she would remove herself from the situation and calm herself down in a different room. Even if she was in Wal-Mart and heard a man behind her talking with a deep voice, she would excuse herself from the line and calm herself down in the Wal-Mart bathroom. While she was walking away, she would engage in self-talk to help keep her anxiety down. Some of her self-talk would be, "I'm okay, I'm okay," "I'm safe, I'm safe," "Just make it to the bathroom, just make it to the bathroom."

As time went on and other things related to her domestic violence experience were addressed, her coping tools changed. If she was at church and heard a man talking in a deep voice, she would take a step back from where he was, force herself to stay in the same room, scribble on a piece of paper to get some of her anxiety out, and do deep breathing. If her anxiety didn't reduce, she would use a grounding technique or talk to a friend. At first, those coping tools didn't work and she would leave the room, which was the best choice since her anxiety didn't decrease. As time went on and she strived to use those coping tools, she was able to stay in the room with the person who had the deep voice.

Once Stephanie mastered being able to manage her anxiety using coping tools when she heard a man's deep voice, she was willing to take things a step further by looking at the man. This entire time, Stephanie would immediately look down at the floor when she heard a man's deep voice. Now she wanted to be able to continue looking up. After practice, she was able to not only look up, but was able to look at the man who had the deep voice. After adding several more coping tools to her repertoire, she was able hold a conversation with a man who had a deep voice as long as another person was also engaged in the conversation. Her next goal is to be able to talk with a man who has a deep voice one-on-one and to consistently look him in the eyes while managing her anxiety.

As you see, for Stephanie, identifying her trigger helped her figure out why she was having panic attacks and she was able to find coping tools to help her manage her panic attacks. Stephanie had other triggers that caused her to have panic attacks, and she was able to identify those and use coping tools to reduce her panic attacks overall.

Stephanie was able to finally reach her goal of maintaining eye contact while engaging in a conversation with a man who had a deep voice, and managing her anxiety throughout the interaction.

What to do:

1. Write down triggers, be very specific. For example, the smell of Lucky perfume, men with beards, walking alone at night time, hearing a certain ring tone, etc.

2. Write down your reaction to those triggers. Some may experience intense feelings when doing number one or two. Remind yourself

that knowledge is power and that you are in a safe place.

3. Write down ways to avoid your triggers until you find effective coping tools. For example, change the channel if rape scenes are a trigger, avoid neighborhoods if a certain house is a trigger, avoid fireworks if loud sounds are a trigger, etc.

    If you can't avoid a trigger, write down ways to compromise.

    Here are a few examples:

    A. Felling anxious in large crowds but you have to go grocery shopping, go early in the morning or late at night when there aren't large crowds.

    B. Feeling uncomfortable in mixed crowds, go with several friends you feel safe with.

C. Being on a crowded bus is a trigger, try to walk, wait for a less crowded bus, listen to music to zone everyone out on the bus, or sit or stand close to the exit door or driver to feel safer.

4. When you are ready, and you will know when you are, use some of these other coping tools listed in the book to help when faced with a trigger to take control of your reaction.

Remember, knowledge is power, and knowing your triggers is the first step in overcoming them and leading a healthier life.

Notes

Chapter Five

Regular Physical Activity

Benefits: Decrease Depression, Decrease Anxiety, Redirects Anger

After experiencing abuse, some may have moments of having a clear mind, and other times having a cloudy mind. It seems as if we go through the motions of life, or for some, refuse to engage in life. Restoring our clear mind and functioning as a healthy and active participant in the world can be a challenge. Remind yourself that there is a way we can get our clear and focused mind back, physical activity.

For some of us, when we think of exercise, we cringe because it takes energy and work and think we have to go to the gym five times a week. It can sometimes be intimidating to exercise, especially if we have never exercised or haven't exercised in years. Before marking this tool out, please read further. You might be surprised by simple things you can do around the house to keep your body in motion.

First, let's take a look at how physical activity can benefit our mind related to trauma. According to a study done by the Department of Exercise Science at the University of Georgia, exercise not only increases the heart rate, but it also pumps more oxygen to the brain.[4] The more oxygen we get to our brain, the more clear our mind can become.

BrainHQ informs that exercise releases hormones that aid in the growth of brain cells. It also shared that when we dance, it uses several parts of our brain, coordination, rhythm, and strategy. This shows that different exercises benefit us differently. The article goes on to say that when we exercise in the morning, it "prepares you for mental stresses for the rest of the day" (Physical Exercise for the Brain Health by BrainHQ).[5]

Reader's Digest takes things a step further and states, "exercise may help lift your mood." The release of serotonin and dopamine (chemicals in the brain that influence our mood) are increased through exercise. (6 Ways Exercise Makes Your Brain Better by Reader's Digest)[6]

Realizing how exercise increases oxygen to the brain can prepare us for mental stress and increases hormones that influence our mood, we can see that exercise is extremely beneficial in our recovery from trauma and abuse. Doing physical activity also influences our self-esteem. When we do healthy things for ourselves, such as physical activity, we feel good about ourselves, it boosts our confidence and we begin to see ourselves in a more positive light.

Let's take a look at the type and frequency of physical activity. As stated earlier in the chapter, at first look, physical activity can be scary and intimidating if we haven't done it for years. Physical activity doesn't have to be high intensity, it can be low-key. It can be going for a walk in your neighborhood, or start out by doing five jumping jacks, five pushups, and five lunges in your living room. For more ideas, take a look on YouTube for videos on how to do low-key work outs for tem minutes. Again, physical activity doesn't have to be five times a week for an hour at the gym. It can literally be in your living room for 10-20 minutes. Take a look at **What to do** on the next page for a breakdown on the steps you can take to help improve your self-esteem and better manage your anger, depression, and anxiety.

What to do:

1.   Intentionally set time aside to exercise. It can be once a week, twice a week, or daily if your schedule allows it.

2.   Choose an exercise, walking, jogging, dancing, gym exercises, etc. Some may not be able to exercise due to health concerns. I would encourage getting in contact with a personal trainer. Many of them will give an upfront session for free and can give suggestions on exercises you can do. It's also best to consult with your primary care doctor if you are interested in exercising but have health concerns that may prohibit you.

3. Stay committed to exercising during the time you set aside.

4. Remind yourself that every time you exercise, you're making a healthy decision in your recovery process.

5. Have fun and continue acknowledging that you're making a healthy choice.

Notes

Chapter Six

Spirituality

<u>Benefits</u>: Manage the Following: Depression, Anger, Anxiety, Flashbacks

The mental, emotional, physical, and spiritual aspects of our life all intertwine. If you notice, throughout the book, we touch on each of these fundamental parts that make up who we are. Even if you don't believe or practice a spiritual approach, there are benefits and lessons we can learn from diverse spiritual orientations. There are practices, prayers, and quotes that can bring peace, joy, and restoration. Below are a few quotes from the Bible, other resources, and a prayer. If the words below don't bring support, I encourage you to find your own quote, Bible verse, or story that brings you peace and inspiration to keep moving forward.

Bible Verses

Psalm 34:4 (KJV) *I sought the Lord and He heard me and delivered me from all my fears.*

Psalm 139:14 (KJV) *We are fearfully and wonderfully made.*

Jeremiah 29:10b-11 (MSG) *I'll show up and take care of you as I promised and bring you back home. I know what I'm doing. I have it all planned out-plans to take care of you, not abandon you, plans to give you the future you hope for.*

Joshua 1:9 (MSG) *Haven't I commanded you? Strength! Courage! Don't be timid; don't get discouraged. God, your God, is with you every step you take.*

Mark 11:24 (ESV) *Whatever you ask in prayer, believe that you have received it, and it will be yours.*

I Peter 5:10 (ESV) *And after you have suffered a little while, the God of all grace, who has called you to his eternal glory in Christ, will Himself restore, confirm, strengthen, and establish you.*

Isaiah 40:31 (KJV) *But they that wait upon the LORD shall renew their strength; they shall mount up with wings as eagles; they shall run, and not be weary; and they shall walk, and not faint.*

(Scripture marked KJV are from the King James Version.
Scripture marked MSG are from The Message: The Bible in Contemporary English.
Scripture marked ESV are from the English Standard Version.)

Quotes

"Don't judge yourself by what others did to you."

—C. Kennedy, Omorphi

"Sticks and stones can break your bones, but words can never hurt you...unless you believe them." —Charles F. Glassman

"The enemy doesn't stand a chance when the victim decides to survive." —Rae Smith

"Like any trauma, recovering from abuse takes time." —Unknown

"Forgiveness liberates the soul. It removes fear. That is why it is such a powerful weapon." —Morgan Freeman

"The past can hurt, but the way I see it, you can either run from it or learn from it." —Rafiki

"What defines us is how well we rise after falling." —Bob Hoskins

Prayer

"We pray for healing. We pray for deep comfort. We pray that You will restore what has been stolen and broken. While You do not alter history, You reveal Your love in the present and

the future. What seems hopelessly shattered, in

You can be redeemed.

    Yes, there is great pain in this world. There

is injustice. There is evil. We turn to You and cry

out for help and healing. God, You are good and

loving and also all-powerful. Yet, You have risked

giving humans the right to choose how we will

love. Some choose evil. For those who are victims

of others' vile deeds, we ask You for grace and

healing. For those who have suffered, come to us

tenderly and with overwhelming and powerful

love. We join Jesus and borrow his words, Be freed

from your suffering. God, Heal us of abuse, in Jesus'

name." —Mark Herringshaw[7]

What to do:

1. Find a Bible verse, quote, or prayer that brings you comfort, encouragement, or motivation.

2. Purposefully say it out loud every morning and every night. When we say things out loud, it penetrates our minds more efficiently.

3. Keep the Bible verse, quote, or prayer close by to be able to read if needed throughout the day.

Notes

_____

_____

_____

_____

_____

_____

_____

_____

_____

_____

Chapter Seven

Thought Stopping

Benefits: Decrease Length of the Following: Flashbacks, Unhealthy Thoughts

Imagine being bored at school or at work. You're sitting at your desk, daydreaming of what you could be doing if you were at home or spending time with your best friends. Your mind is wandering deeply into your imagination.

Suddenly, someone slams a book on your desk. What happens to that daydream? What happens to your mind?

The daydream immediately disappears and your mind is jolted. You may even let out a scream from surprise and fear. Our daydream dissimilates and we are back in reality.

Thought stopping is the same concept. We can get trapped in reliving a past event and seem to become stuck there. We may think about bad things happening to us or someone else throughout the day, or we may dwell on how bad life is treating us. Whichever category we fall under, our thoughts are in our control.

We can control what we think about, resulting in us either leading anxious and depression-filled lives, or us leading peaceful and happy lives.

What to do:

1. Think of a relaxing or happy memory. If it's hard to think of a relaxing or happy memory, create your own or find a funny joke. As long as the thought is something that brings you energy, drive, peace, or happiness, it will work.

2. Write down a few words that will remind you of your relaxing thought. You can write it on a 3x5 card or in your phone (most phones have an app that allows you to type in notes). If you have time, write down the entire memory, thought, or joke. Another option is to record it in your phone (most phones today have a recording app).

3. When you begin to think negatively, take note of it. This may be difficult for some. Act as if you are a friend who is inspecting your thoughts. As a friend, would you think those thoughts are healthy or depriving? If they are healthy, great! If they are depriving, go to the next step.

4. Think of your relaxing or happy thought. If you can't remember, it's okay. Pull out your 3x5 card or phone and read or listen to the

relaxing and happy thought, memory, or joke you chose.

When we first start using the thought stopping technique, like any behavior we are trying to change, it's not easy. Many of us have spent years daydreaming, imagining, or dwelling on unhealthy thoughts, causing us to experience anxiety, depression, guilt, and many other depriving emotions. It goes back to baby steps.

There are times when clients have told me that they had negative thoughts all day, but at the end of the day, they remembered to pull out their 3x5 card to switch their thoughts. Even though most of the day was spent focusing on negative thoughts and they succeeded only once, we still celebrated.

We celebrated because they made an improvement. Yes, thought stopping was used only once during the day, but guess what, the next day and the day after that, it became easier for them to remember to use the thought stopping technique. Before they knew it, they could recognize triggers to their thoughts and delete those thoughts before they even have a chance to run rampant in their mind. You can do it, just give it a try.

The power over your thoughts is yours, you just have to realize it and use it.

Notes

_____

_____

_____

_____

_____

_____

_____

_____

_____

Chapter Eight

Turtle It

Benefits: Manage the Following: Self-Doubt, Anxiety, Stress, Anger

Are there times when self-doubt, anxiety, stress, and feeling tired seem to run your life? Try Turtle It.

Turtle It is an interesting Dialectical Behavior Therapy technique that works with children and adults. With children, we are able to literally pretend we are a turtle and tuck into our shell to refocus. I've noticed that most adults I work with prefer to not pretend to tuck into a shell physically while in session, but many do seem to enjoy tucking mentally to gain a moment of clarity.

Let's take a look at Lindsey's experience and how she used Turtle It to control her stress and anxiety.

Lindsey is a single mother with two boys. She works full time at a car dealership as a secretary. She has worked there for three weeks and is somewhat getting the hang of things. She has a history of anxiety when in a large crowd and is easily stressed. Although no one has made any concerning remarks, Lindsey many times, loses sleep in fear that she may get fired because she still doesn't fully know all of her job responsibilities.

The car dealership she is working for is having a grand sale tomorrow. The night before the sale, Lindsey has a nightmare about the sale, resulting in her waking up in a night sweat and not sleeping the rest of the night.

The next morning, she gets her two boys ready for school, takes them to the bus stop, and returns home to get herself ready for work.

As the clock ticks closer to her needing to be at work, her anxiety get's higher and higher. Racing thoughts shoot through her mind of being unable to keep up with the demands of the customers, which may result in her getting fired, then she will be unable to pay bills and buy food. Her mind then races to the thought of her and her sons not having a place to live.

As she drives to work, those racing thoughts continue to spiral out of control, along with her anxiety. She wonders if her and her boys will become homeless. She imagines having to move back in with her parents who will criticize her parenting. She thinks of how the boys' father will then criticize her for being unable to keep a job and will call her an unfit mother. Lindsey slowly drives into her parking spot and continues to have these thoughts swarming in her mind.

Her day at work begins and she does her best to keep up with the busyness of the grand sale. She barely makes it to lunchtime and has to go outside for a smoke break to calm her nerves. She's able to calm them down for a brief moment, when an auto mechanic who she met on the first day, begins making sexual comments towards her. She ignores his comments and returns to work. An hour later, the same auto mechanic walks by her in anger for being ignored and whispers sexual comments towards her again.

Lindsey tells him to leave her alone. He then makes remarks about him forcing her to engage in sexual activities with him if she continues to say no.

Just then a car salesman walks to Lindsey's desk to ask her to complete needed paperwork related to a sale. The auto mechanic quickly walks away, but not before rubbing his hand on Lindsey's arm. Lindsey freezes and memories of her being raped flood her mind. She is looking at the car salesman, but doesn't fully hear him.

The last two hours of work, Lindsey goes through the motions, but is not completely present mentally. She is emotionally numb. Several times, sales representatives and other secretaries had to remind Lindsey to do simple tasks because her mind was foggy.

The work day finally ends and she picks her two sons up from the bus stop, with her mind still foggy. Her two sons ask what's for dinner, and she replies, "I don't know."

The boys can tell something is different with their mother and comes to her with every little problem wanting their mother's attention. Her two sons begin to argue over what to watch on TV and the youngest comes to her bedroom crying. She immediately tells herself, *I'm tired, I can't do this right now. I'm just going to Turtle It.*

Lindsey takes a moment to weigh out the pros and cons of the decision she is about to make and finally chooses to reach out to her parents for help. She packs two bags for her sons to stay the night at her parents. Her parents come and she tells them that she needs an evening alone to work through some things. Her parents make several negative remarks about her parenting.

Lindsey does her best to ignore her parents' comments and kisses her two boys goodnight. As soon as her parents and sons leave, Lindsey slumps to the floor and cries. She cries out of frustration and anxiety. She is able to think about the techniques she learned when she was in therapy after her rape. She spends the rest of the evening working through her thoughts and feelings related to the day's events. Lindsey is able to recognize that she could have used the Turtle It Technique several times throughout the day and if she had, she could have made an immediate decision to report the mechanic guy.

Lindsey did other coping skills that evening. She drank hot tea, wrote in her journal, listened to music, and took a hot bubble bath.

The next day, she felt rejuvenated and was able to confidently report the mechanic to her boss.

Her boss said he would look into things. When she left his office, her anxiety rose and thoughts raced through her mind. She began to wonder if her boss believed her. If he didn't believe her, what would the mechanic do?

Fear struck her as she realized that the mechanic would know it was her who said something and may try to harm her or worse, follow her home. As her mind continued to race, she remembered Turtle It. She decided to give herself permission to slow down and wait and see what would happen to the mechanic. About an hour later, her boss came and informed her that the mechanic was fired.

Lindsey decided to use Turtle It more often throughout her day to better manage her anxiety and stress.

What to do:

1. Recognize when you are feeling threatened, afraid, tired, angry, stressed, or anxious.

2. Give yourself permission to remove yourself from the situation or stressor.

   If you're unable to remove yourself from the situation, give yourself permission to slow down to solve the problem or wait to get more information.

3. Remember, turtles have a hard outer shell to protect against rain and harsh sunlight. Imagine having an emotional or mental shell that protects you from negative things others may say or do towards you.

4. While you use Turtle It as your mental shell, use other coping tool to rejuvenate and clear your mind. For example, Stephanie cried, worked through her thoughts and feelings, drank hot tea, wrote in her journal, listened to music, and took a bubble bath.

5. Take a moment to acknowledge that you are safe and calm in your mental shell.

6. Identify pros and cons of decisions and make the healthiest choice for you. Sometimes it may require reaching out to a trusted friend to help with the decision-making process.

7. When you're ready, come out of your mental shell and be a productive adult.

8. Acknowledge that you made a healthy decision to Turtle It.

9. Keep in mind that there are times when we must be assertive to take care of a situations

and there are times when using the Turtle It Technique is the healthiest choice. We have to take each situation as they come to decide which is healthiest, assertiveness or Turtle It.

Notes

_____

_____

_____

_____

_____

_____

_____

Chapter Nine

Healthy Verses Unhealthy Decisions

Benefits: Change Every Aspect of Our Lives Drastically

Many of us can become so warped in life, until it's hard to see our way out. Oftentimes when abuse happens, it causes us to experience a whirlwind of negative thoughts, emotions, and actions. Then one day we look up and don't even recognize who we've become. Or maybe we've felt that we've always had a warped mindset, but was unaware of our actions until someone pointed them out. Whichever category you fall in, just know that you are able to change who you are and live a healthy life.

The first thing we have to do before making a decision is to ask one simple question: "Is this healthy or unhealthy?" Now for those who are like me (who can be a smart aleck), we can find something healthy in any decision, even if the decision is obviously unhealthy. It's when we're sincere and truly want to lead a healthy and successful life, we are able to honestly and truthfully answer this question.

Let's explore the question, "Is this healthy or unhealthy," further by looking at Ruthie.

Ruthie is a smart, intelligent, and very optimistic woman. She was able to find the good in any situation. She was also sexually abused when she was a child. Throughout her recovery, she kept an upbeat appearance, while on the inside was hurting, depressed, and anxious.

Her perpetrator was a distant relative who she saw once or twice a year at family functions. She chose to never tell her family of the abuse. She feared what her family may say or do. She also resisted sharing because she felt that the perpetrator was, at the time, being a "typical teenage boy" who was curious about sex and body parts.

After a recent family function, she was told that her perpetrator asked another family member for her phone number. She felt angry and anxious after realizing that he had her number, however, hopeful that he wouldn't call. A few weeks later, he used it, and they initially spoke briefly over the phone. As time went on, they began to talk more and more and she felt that things were okay because he was being nice. She also noticed that her flashbacks and nightmares soon returned. Soon, the conversation turned sexual and she became uncomfortable. She began ignoring his calls, resulting in him becoming angry and sending hateful texts. A few months later he finally stopped texting.

Ruthie resumed therapy and learned several techniques to help with her depression, anxiety, stress, nightmares, and flashbacks that had returned. It was getting close to the holidays and of course, another family function. Ruthie received a phone call from her perpetrator a couple of weeks before the family get-together. He apologized for his previous texts and was very kind towards Ruthie.

After the phone call, Ruthie had mixed emotions and wasn't sure what to do if he called again. A few days later, her perpetrator called again. While on the phone, Ruthie noticed her anxiety was high. She began to have flashbacks while talking to him. Even though her perpetrator seemed harmless and they were having a good conversation, she asked herself, is this healthy or unhealthy?

It was difficult for her to decide. It seemed healthy because they were laughing and having a good conversation. It also seemed unhealthy because her anxiety was high and she was having flashbacks just by hearing his voice. She realized that talking to her perpetrator on the phone was unhealthy for her because she was having flashbacks and experiencing high anxiety. She decided to get off the phone.

A few days later, her perpetrator called again. This time, Ruthie didn't answer. As she laid the phone back down, ignoring the call, she felt gratification knowing she made a healthy choice for herself. It in turn, boosted her self-esteem and confidence. She realized that by making this single, healthy choice, she was more than capable of making other healthy choices that would positively influence her future.

What to do:

1. Before making a decision, ask yourself, "Is this healthy or unhealthy?"
2. List the pros of each decision. List the cons of each decision.
3. Make the best decision for yourself.
4. If you are have difficulty making the healthiest decision, talk about it with a trusted person.

It's also encouraged to ask, "Was that a healthy or unhealthy decision?" afterwards. Some may wonder, "Why ask after I already made the decision? The decision and act have been made." Great question and insight.

Life is a learning process. At the time, things may seem like a good idea. Like in Ruthie's case, at first she thought talking to her perpetrator was okay, and soon realized it wasn't a good idea and ignored his next call.

Examples: Answer these for yourself, "Are these healthy or unhealthy decisions?"

1. Laying in bed all week doing nothing when it's not due to a health-related issue.

2. Calling an ex who you have a history of arguing with during the majority of conversations.

3. Being on a diet and craving a cheeseburger, but instead drinking a fruit shake and eating a fruit salad.

4. Canceling a workout class to watch five hours of your favorite show on Netflix.

5. Reminiscing about past drug use.

6. Making a list of how you can better your life.

Notes

_____

_____

_____

_____

_____

_____

_____

_____

Chapter Ten

Sense of Touch to Self Soothe

Benefits: Reduces the Following: Anger, Anxiety, Panic Attacks

In Chapter Three, we discussed grounding, a technique that we can use when we feel anxious or angry, to help calm us down. There are many different tools that fall under that category of grounding which we can use to reduce our anxiety and anger. Some might listen to music while others might watch their favorite funny movie to manage their anger and anxiety. Many people intentionally smell lavender when feeling anxious because the fragrance is relaxing. How many of us have turned to food to manage our anxiety? Our senses can soothe us when feeling anxious or angry.

Pauline is a great example to show how our senses can help manage those challenging feelings. Pauline experienced intense anxiety when she had to go to stores. She found something unique that soothed her when her anxiety began to rise. She used a piece of wool from an old blanket her grandmother made. The texture made her feel happy and knowing she had something from her grandmother brought her comfort.

One weekend, Pauline went out of town to visit family and went into a dollar store to get a few items. When she got into line, there was a long line and tension of the customers was rising because of the wait. Pauline felt her anxiety rising. She slipped her hand in her pocket and began rubbing that piece of wool with her fingers. She focused on the texture. She focused on how soft it felt. She focused on how warm it felt. She was able to reduce her anxiety long enough for her to purchase her items and leave the store.

There are many more things we can use to engage our senses of touch to better reduce our anger and anxiety. There's no reason to over think what will or won't work. It truly can be something extremely simple, as long as it's something that's healthy and brings you comfort. I encourage you to find what works for you. Finding the right thing for you can be a trial and error process, so don't give up on this tool at the first go around.

What to do:

1. Find something that stimulates your senses and brings relaxation to your mind. It needs

to be small enough for you to be able to carry everywhere you go.

2.   Keep that item with you at all times.

3.   Notice when you begin to feel anxious or angry.

4.   Use your sense to focus on the item to help soothe you.

It's important that we not only know how to use this tool when in the community, but also when we are at home. We can use our sense of touch with other senses as a coping tool as well. A few suggestions you can do while at home are below:

1.   Run your hands under cold water, then hot water, and focus on how your hands feel under the water with the different temperatures (make sure the water isn't too hot for touch).

2.   Take a shower.

3. Rub your hands with lotion and smell the lotion.

4. Look at a serene or calming picture while rubbing soft fabric.

5. Create a peaceful place in your home. Go there often to relax and embrace peace of mind.

6. Focus on the slow swiping motion of your finger across your phone as you look through relaxing or calming photos.

Notes

_____

_____

_____

_____

_____

Chapter Eleven

Volunteer

<u>Benefits</u>: Manage Depression

Over the years, there have been many research teams who have explored what influences us to lead healthy and happy lives. Eating right, getting plenty of sleep, and exercise are things most of us know, but what some may not know is the influence volunteering has on our mood.

In the UK, Dr. Suzanne Richards reviewed studies from the past 20 years on volunteering. She published her findings in the BMC Public Health. What she found was volunteering is associated with lowering depression.[8]

In Harvard Health Publications, Stephanie Watson shares that, "Studies have shown that volunteering helps people who donate their time feel more socially connected, thus warding off loneliness and depression."[9]

Lastly, Dr. Nicole Anderson from Rotman Research Institute at Baycrest Health Sciences, reviewed studies over the past 45 years about volunteering. She shared that, "feeling appreciated or needed as a volunteer appears to reduce depressive symptoms." [10]

There are so many places to volunteer. If you like painting houses, Habitat for Humanity; if you enjoy animals, local animal shelters; if you enjoy interacting with children, volunteer at a youth shelter; if you want to be a mentor, Big Brother's Big Sister's; if you want to support the sick, volunteer at a local hospital; if you like socializing, volunteer for an arts festival; if you want to support the homeless, volunteer at a food pantry or soup kitchen. Take a look within your community and find a volunteer opportunity that fits you.

What to do:

1. Think of a volunteer opportunity you would like to do and are passionate about.
2. Find an organization that offers the activity you're interested in and gather information on the sign-up process.
3. Set aside a specific time that fits your schedule to volunteer with the organization. It can be daily, weekly, bi-weekly, or monthly.
4. Sign up to volunteer, letting them know what days and time you are committed to being there.
5. Go on the day you signed up to volunteer and have fun!

6. Remind yourself that you are making a healthy choice.

For those who have intense anxiety and may find it difficult to volunteer out in the community, it's okay; there are other low-key volunteer opportunities. Below are a list of a few ideas for volunteering:

1. Drive a friend to an appointment.

2. Babysit a friend's child.

3. Write an encouraging letter to someone.

4. Help an elderly neighbor.

5. Cook a meal and take it to someone who is sick.

Notes

_____

_____

_____

_____

_____

_____

_____

_____

_____

Appendix

1. Buczynski, R., Two Chemical Reactions that Happen in the Brain During Trauma. https://www.nicabm.com/trauma-two-chemical-reactions-that-happen-in-th-brain-during-trauma/ Video Retrieved February 27, 1016.

2. Lyubomirsky, S. (2008). The How of Happiness: A Scientific Approach to Getting the Life You Want. New York: Penguin Press.

3. Merriam Webster. Retrieved February 27, 2016, from Http://www.merriam-webster.com/dictionary/trigger

4. Tomporowski, P.D. (2003). Effects of Acute Bouts of Exercise on Cognition. Acta Psychologica, 112, 297-324.

5. Physical Exercise for Brain Health. Retrieved February 27, 2016, from www.brainhq.com/brain-resources/everyday-brain-fitness/physical-exercise

6. Six Ways Exercise Makes Your Brain Better. Retrieved February 27, 2016, from www.rd.com/health/fitness/6-ways-exercise-makes-your-brain-better/

7. Herringshaw, M.. Sexual Abuse- a Prayer for Victims. Posted to http://www.beliefnet.com/columnists/prayerpl ainandsimple/2011/07/a-prayer-for-victims-of-sexual-abuse.html#VoB5hSA6rhzcwfou.99

8. Dickens, C., Jenkinson, C., Jones, K., Richards, S., Rogers, M., Taylor, R., Thompson-Coon, J.et al.: Is volunteering a public intervention? A systemic review and meta-analysis of the health and

survival of volunteers. BMC Public Health 13, 773 (2013).

9. Watson, S., (Published 2013. Updated 2015). Volunteering May be Good for Body and Mind. Retrieved February 16, 2016, from www.health.harvard.edu/blog/volunteering-may-be-good-for-body-and-mind-201306266428

10. Baycrest Health Sciences, Rotman Research Institute. (2014). Evidence Mounting that Older Adults Who Volunteer are Happier, Healthier [Press Release] Retrieved from www.baycrest.org/mart-aging/mental-health-sa/evidence-mounting-that-older-adults-who-volunteer-are-happier-healthier/

About the Author

Tiffani Dilworth is a Licensed Certified Professional Counselor residing in Maryland. She started her career working with children and specializing in trauma. Later, she transitioned to working with adults and specializing in trauma related to abuse. She is the Founder of Inspirational Hope LLC, which started out as an online community that promotes support and encouragement to others who've experienced abuse. Tiffani takes great joy in being a Public Speaker who instills hope and inspires others to "keep moving forward." During her events, she focuses on sharing with listeners the importance of them recognizing their self value.

Contact Author

Website:
InspirationalHope.org

E-mail:
Tiffani.Dilworth@InspirationalHope.org

Twitter:
@TiffaniDilworth

Facebook:
Inspirational Hope

Printed in Great Britain
by Amazon

31627780R00058